MBA

Coffee Chats

Thoughtful Advice on
How to Get the Most
Out of Your MBA

Bob Manfreda
Adam Putterman

The Admit

Congratulations! You got into a great business school. Take it in. It's a big accomplishment.

If you're anything like us, when you heard the news, you probably felt a bit tired and absolutely thrilled, and were left wondering: "How can I make the most of this massive investment of time and money?"

It's hard to know because, well, you've never done it before. Furthermore, most of the information available to you is about getting *in* to school. There's not much on what comes next.

Three groups curate nearly everything you'll find on the MBA experience: schools, admissions consultants, and blogs. None of them focus on the Admit. Schools focus on students and are generally biased. Consultants stick almost exclusively to admissions. Blogs make money on advertising via clickbait-y titles that rely on 790 GMATs, catalog profiles, and janky rankings. I'm sure you've noticed.

In the face of so much misinformation, the greatest tool you can wield is the coffee chat.

Coffee chats are simple but candid conversations about life during school. They're an integral part of the MBA experience and will litter your calendar for the next two years. You'll regularly be "grabbing coffee" with fellow students, professors, and recruiters. You will be shocked at what you discover, and only sometimes will you actually drink coffee.

If you haven't had a recent coffee chat yet, it should be the next thing you do. In person is obviously ideal, but remote is still far better than nothing. Even if you're not sure why, make a list of students or grads from your school that you could reach out to. Then ask for twenty to thirty minutes of their time. (If you'd like more advice on how to find someone to talk with, we've included an entire section on this topic towards the back of the book, in Chapter 15.)

Here's how the conversations usually go:

So, tell me about the MBA, any advice you'd recommend?

Yeah, it's amazing. But you're SO busy. You're going to want to be very focused. Only do the things that really matter to you.

Wow, that's great! What were some of your favorite classes?

I loved Negotiations. The professor is incredible. Some people hated it, but I loved it. This one time...

(10 minutes later:) Anything you wish you knew before you started?

I guess I wish I had budgeted better. Definitely make sure you don't run out of money. Also...

These conversations are almost always fun. The person is excited for you and enjoys reminiscing about their experience. But these conversations should also offer personalized advice. You're looking for real talk.

You probably don't have an endless list of contacts to chat with, and most coffee chats are a fairly limited and time-intensive resource. So you want to make sure you don't waste your opportunity. Push your fellow coffee chatter (in the gentlest way possible) towards the questions you most need answered.

This book will save you precious figuring-stuff-out time by answering in advance the most popular questions that come up during these chats. Unsurprisingly, Admits ask many of the same introductory questions in their initial coffee chats.

Once we noticed that the same questions were coming up again and again in chats we were having with recent Admits, we wrote down our answers and passed them along instead of answering them anew every time. We then shared these answers with MBA friends and incorporated their thoughts as well.

This short book is the result. It reflects our personal experiences at Kellogg and Stanford, countless friends' stories, our mentors' advice, and a few other random musings that seem smart. It's our most thoughtful and comprehensive response to the most common Admit question: "How can I make the most of my experience?"

Nothing you read will ever replace the value of one-on-one conversations. But reading this book in advance can supplement and enhance those conversations. This book is your starter content to prep for real coffee chats. It will provide the baseline knowledge you need to ask better, higher-value questions—ones that solicit the personal and subjective responses most useful to you.

Because of our focus on the Admit, there are several topics that are not covered in the book. We purposely left out questions about anything prior to admissions, including GMATs, applications, and deciding between schools. We also won't get tactical on interviews, career choices, or which clubs to join. We provide a relatively light touch on recruiting because it varies from school to school and is constantly evolving. In our opinion, the variability of these topics don't make them well-suited to a book (at least, not one we want to write). Instead, we have addressed some of these issues on our website, mbacoffeechats.com.

This is not a chronological tale of the MBA experience. That's not really our style. We believe those kinds of books are ineffective and unrealistic. The MBA experience is too personal for generic tell-alls.

This book is, well, a coffee chat. With that in mind, feel free to jump around to questions that are most relevant to you. Everyone's situation is a bit different - and always changing. Not all of this advice will apply to you. That's okay.

Ideally, you'll read this now to get a baseline understanding of the experience and then revisit whatever parts feel most salient during your first year. This book covers a range of topics summarized below. Some you may need to know right now, while others will resonate more once you're on campus.

To give you an idea of what to expect, these are the common coffee chat questions we cover:

The Core Experience

1. **What are the classes and academics like?**
   Most Admits have some anxiety around school, usually driven by the ambiguity of the classroom experience. Everyone's different, but some structured self-reflection should help you better understand your situation.
2. **How can I remember everything important?**
   School is expensive. People want to know how to retain most of the value they're shelling out cash for.
3. **What's the best thing you did in school?**
   Almost everyone has a favorite thing they did in school. We think it's less helpful to hear what that specific thing was and more helpful to hear how/why people chose that thing.
4. **What does a week look like?**
   A surprising number of people just want to know how much time they'll spend in class vs. socializing vs. other activities. We try to break this down.

The Top Three Concerns

5. **How can I maintain a strong relationship with my partner?**
   Lots of students come into school with serious romantic partners. If this describes you, surviving school together requires some additional strategizing.

6. **How should I prioritize my time?**

   The most common advice you'll hear is to "prioritize." But what does prioritization look like during an MBA?

7. **How can I grow and get better?**

   We all (hopefully) know the importance of feedback to growth and development. But what are the best strategies for finding it while you're at school?

The Tactical Stuff

8. **Should I get a club leadership role?**

   Every school hype up their clubs, and many students feel compelled to take a leadership role in one of them. What should you consider before signing up?

9. **When should I quit my pre-MBA job?**

   Sometimes people have already decided this themselves, but it's okay if you're not sure how to think through it. Lots of your classmates are in the same boat.

10. **How do I find a pre-MBA internship (if I want one)?**

    Not everyone asks about this, but those who do are usually pretty passionate about it. We think an internship is a best-of-all-worlds option and we love helping people figure it out.

11. **How can I figure out what I want to do?**

    Obviously, a big part of the MBA is the career it leads you to. Sure, you probably had a career "story" that you told in your application. But most MBA students are still exploring a couple of options and want to know how they can do this most effectively.

12. **Should I start a business?**

    Starting a business while you're in school is an

increasingly popular path, and there are strong opinions in favor of and against doing so.

The Meta Layer

13. **Miscellaneous tips.**
    In this section we included a grab bag of random advice that didn't fit in our responses to the previous questions.
14. **What to ask and how to ask it.**
    To get the most from these chats, you'll need to both find the right people and ask the right questions.
15. **How to find people to chat with.**
    You'll generally begin by reaching out to friendly first contacts. After that, to keep the momentum, you'll want to know how to identify the right "strangers" and how to reach out to them properly.

One final note before we dive in. If you haven't noticed already, this book was written by two people—Bob and Adam. Instead of switching back and forth between speakers, we'll refer to ourselves as "we" or "I" throughout the book to keep things simple.

Without further ado, let's have a coffee chat.

PART 1

THE CORE EXPERIENCE

CHAPTER 1

What are the classes and academics like?

Real Student Answer

"I remember the first week of school we did a team-building activity where we were using LEGOs. I called home laughing about having bought the most expensive LEGO set of my life. There's definitely some goofy aspects of school, in part because, at least for me, so much of the experience was about soft skills. Those are harder to learn in class (but the school still tried), so there ended up being a fair amount of experiential learning. All in all, nothing from class was really mind-blowing, and to a certain degree it can all be found online, but it was definitely a lot easier to learn in the school environment. And the classmates were a huge part of it. Even in non-case classes, it seemed we always

had someone with direct experience on the topic who could add some behind-the-scenes color. I learned a lot from the different questions my classmates asked. Somewhat related... I definitely found it a bit weird that there were 'participation points.' I never really understood what that meant, but in the end, it also didn't seem like it was that big of a deal."

There are a lot of variations to this question, but the subtext is usually the same: the person wants to know how hard they'll need to hustle, and if it even matters. Most Admits have been away from school for a few years, and the prospect of returning seems to create some anxiety.

So does school really matter? School—that is, the academic part of the two years you'll be spending at a university—is often joked about as the least important part of the MBA experience. If that's true for you, fine. But don't default into that option. It's a reflection of popular priorities, not an infallible truth.

In short, there are two reasons school matters.

1. Because You're Paying For It... Right?

Some people will probably feel this question is ridiculous. "Of course school matters, the MBA is an expensive academic degree," they'd say. Others are probably rolling their eyes right now. The truth is, many MBA students value the network they build, the job opportunities it creates, the student experience, and many other aspects far more than the academics. If this is disappointing, hopefully you picked a school where this is less true. Regardless, you are paying a lot of money to a school, so it'd be good to get some academic value. At least we think so.

2. More Importantly, Academics Matter Because Of Their Sheer Volume Of Time

In any given week, you'll probably spend 20+ hours physically sitting in a classroom (or in front of an online lecture). You'll spend additional time completing assignments and preparing for class (remember homework?). In other words, it will essentially become a replacement for your full-time job. And while your job may not have been the most important thing in your life either, it likely had a significant impact on your happiness. Point being, if you are unwilling to think strategically about your academic responsibilities, you won't be able to maximize your MBA experience.

After discussing the importance of school, most Admits move on to asking the second variation of this question: "How hard will I have to work?"

Unfortunately, there is no one-size-fits-all answer. For most people, academic effort is a personal choice. There is usually a lower bound that you'll want to understand: the minimum required effort (MRE—why not create a new acronym? Everyone else in the business world seems to do it). The MRE offers a general idea of what will be required in terms of time and effort. Until you take your first set of exams, you probably won't really know what your MRE is. But here are a few questions that can help provide some guidance beforehand.

1. Does Your School Have Grade Non-disclosure?

First, we need to establish the rules of the road. If your school does not have grade non-disclosure, then the MRE is governed by how the employer you are interested in working for during or after school will judge your performance. However, if your school has grade non-disclosure, then the MRE is set at a much lower bar. It's determined either by your pride (this often diminishes the longer you're in school) or the point at which the school will kick you out or apply restrictions to your other activities or aid.

2. Are You A Native English Speaker? Or, If You're Not Studying In An English-speaking Country, A Native Speaker Of That Country's Primary Language?

All of your classmates will be smart. Most will have good ideas. But those who have to communicate in a foreign language are at a disadvantage. Exams, timed assignments, and qualitative assessments will depend a lot on your language skills. In class, participation grades require that you keep up and chime in. It's harder to speak up when you're not just struggling with what but also how to do so.

3. Have You Studied Business Or Something Quantitative?

If you're familiar with many of the topics typically taught in business school, you'll obviously be at an inherent advantage. If you test out of the core classes, it means you'll likely be able to take classes you are more interested in. Even if you never studied business, though, if you were a math/engineering/sciences student with a quantitative bent, you shouldn't have issues with any of the mechanics and will be able to focus on the content without many problems. A balance sheet is much less complex than quantum mechanics.

4. Do You Come From A Feeder Background, E.G., Consulting Or Finance?

There's a way of speaking and interacting that is somewhat unique to business management. "Similar-to-me" bias is real. If you've previously worked in a professional services field full of MBA alumni, you'll simply "fit" the MBA system a bit more comfortably. This is about culture fit and identity, not how well you'll respond to the actual MBA coursework. It's not a good thing, but it remains a reality at most schools. It's worth pointing out that this "culture" encompasses more than just professional training. It can extend to the social realm as well.

5. Are You In A Relationship?

Presuming monogamy (but hey, you do you), this means you'll have one less major distraction. When many of your classmates are navigating personal life questions or trying to meet someone, you're more likely to be enjoying a movie with your partner and getting a good night's sleep. Obviously, every relationship is unique, but being in a relationship often simplifies things. One obvious exception: if you have kids, you'll have plenty of distractions.

6. Have You Decided Not To Pursue The More Competitive Job Fields?

Similar to the relationship question, this is also about distractions. If you're flying out for interviews or have an overwhelmingly robust career coffee chat schedule, it will take away from your ability to focus on academics. Not only will you have less time for school, you'll also be less effective at it. This may vary over time and from school to school, but the most time-sucking industries to prep for are usually finance and consulting.

THE TAKEAWAY

In sum, if you said yes to all the above, school will not be a challenge. In fact, you'll probably be surprised at how easy it will be. To put things more explicitly: if you complete all of your assignments, you will likely be in the top quarter of your class. If you complete the bare minimums, you'll still pass. Fact is, you have a huge number of advantages.

Even if you said no to a couple of the items, you're still in pretty good shape. The questions are in order of importance. If you're a native English speaker with a quant bent, you're probably looking at a relatively low-effort academic experience even if you don't come from a feeder background. It will likely be easier for you to participate in class than many international students, and you may pick up accounting concepts more quickly than your peers from a non-feeder-background.

If you said no to most of the questions above, then school might be a bit more challenging. At a minimum, expect that school will take a bit more effort. This doesn't mean you're not as smart as your classmates. It just means that you'll have a steeper learning curve. If you'd like, you might want to opt into any prep resources the school provides.

It's worth pointing out, however, that we have literally NEVER heard of a student who failed out of school despite being fully engaged. There's plenty to stress about in life, but this shouldn't be it. Occasionally, students who are also starting a business or working full time might be asked to leave school, but in our experience, this always happens for reasons outside of the classroom.

Most conversations on the topic of schoolwork stop here, but we believe there's an important third variation to the question: "How can I most effectively manage academics?"

You can't escape school. So you might as well be smart about it. Think strategically about how you use or don't use the academic time provided to you. Here are a few tips to keep in mind.

The first three are especially relevant for people who will not struggle with school. The last three might be more helpful for someone who finds school to be more challenging.

1. Grades Should Correlate To Your Interest In The Topic, Not Your Performance.

Don't think about grades like you did in undergrad. An A+ in a class you don't care about is a tragic waste of your time. And time is the most valuable resource during your MBA. Especially if you have grade non-disclosure, feel free to get a low grade in mandatory classes you don't care about. Allocate the time you save towards subjects more intrinsically valuable to you. Go deep in the class you really care about by meeting with the professor or finding extra reading.

2. Pick Classes Based On What Topically Interests You.

Building on the above, drive towards your areas of interest. This may feel like a "duh" statement, but tons of people instinctively flock towards a few popular classes. If you're in an auction or similar system (some schools make you "bid" on classes), you'll have to allocate a ton of points towards these classes. Instead, take some extra time to read class descriptions and figure out what topics seem most interesting. Use popular opinions or professor reviews to avoid really bad classes, but otherwise prioritize topics you care about. The one exception to this might be a class with a "star professor," but they better be a genuine star if you're going to take a course on something you're not even interested in.

3. Timebox Your Work.

Especially if academics are easier for you, give yourself time limits. For example, tell yourself, *"I'll spend sixty minutes on accounting then stop, even if the assignment isn't complete."* This will force you to become more efficient over time. Also, if you work on something for sixty minutes, chances are you've done enough to learn the lessons it provides. That's the actual goal, not completion for completion's sake. It's easy to spiral far more time into a homework assignment than the value you gain from it. If your class is using the case method, you should also time box class prep. Don't let it take over your life.

4. Take Advantage Of Office Hours.

If school is harder for you, take advantage of the magical but often underutilized resource that is "office hours." Professors love talking about their work and are often tremendously helpful. With office hours, you can get efficient, one-on-one support on the toughest (and most interesting) topics.

5. Trade With Your Classmates.

Another pro tip for those who may struggle in school: don't forget your classmates. Many of them will have complementary skill sets. Perhaps you're a wonderful writer and persuasive thinker while they have deep finance experience. Because schools strive for diverse classes, this kind of mix isn't uncommon. Don't hesitate to offer advice and support from your strengths and, in turn, receive advice and support to address your weaknesses.

6. Balance Your Class Load.

Remember, this is a two-year journey. Most schools allow you to choose electives for a significant portion of them. Balance your classes across each academic period that best suits your working style. Some people prefer spikes: really hard periods followed by really easy periods. Others want a steady balance throughout. Design your schedule to suit your preferences.

THE TAKEAWAY

In summary, while school likely won't define your MBA experience, it will take up a large portion of your time. For some people this will be a challenging and rewarding experience. For others, much of it will be routine. Regardless, academics will probably be a significant portion of your week, and as such will affect your experience. Taking the effort to intentionally decide what to spend time on will have a major influence on how well you maximize your MBA experience.

CHAPTER 2

How can I remember everything important?

Real Student Answer

"Ugh... I didn't really do a great job with this. There's just so much happening at school and I didn't really think about this until about halfway through it. I think in some ways you just need to be okay with that. Much of the MBA is skill-based learning, not knowledge based, so I think it's okay to forget some things. However, I did try to regularly talk with a friend of mine at a different school. That helped me be thoughtful and better understand what was happening. In the last month of school, I also sat down and wrote a "This is what I learned" document. Most of it was higher level, but there were a couple detailed frameworks in there as well. I shared it with friends (both in and

out of school) and asked for their thoughts or reactions. We had regular discussions, and they forced me to think more about what I thought I had learned. I continued editing the document throughout the conversations and now have that to reflect on. But I wish I had done a better job throughout school."

In some ways, you can think of your MBA as a buffet: It's infinite food for a finite stomach. But unlike a buffet, the more you retain from your MBA, the better.

You need to think about this before you show up at school. Otherwise, you'll lose valuable information during the hectic first few weeks. It will be really hard to take a step back and capture key learnings if you haven't already thought about how to do so.

Nearly every grad we talked to wishes they had taken better notes. Sitting in a classroom is, for most people, an objectively terrible way to acquire and retain knowledge. One of the best ways to correct for this is to frequently revisit your questions and insights. In the section below, we'll go over four easy, no-nonsense approaches that will help you with this process.

(A quick caveat: If you've never been a diligent note-taker, know that you don't have to take this too far. Just find an approach that works for you and doesn't feel like a chore.)

1. A Project-based Portfolio

You're going to participate in a ridiculous amount of activities in school: case competitions, experiential projects, consulting, social event planning, etc. You will learn new skills, understand new industries, and build amazing things. You'll also forget half of them.

This is where a portfolio can help. You can set an alert every month, reminding you to make a one-pager on every project over that time period—activities, their impact, learnings, challenges, etc. This will be fun to look back on in two years. More importantly, it'll be a game-changer when the time comes for recruiting in some fields, allowing you to go beyond just stating your interests or sharing your passion. Instead, it will allow you to show specific experiences or even work products.

2. Quarterly Peer Reviews

You will be living in a bubble. One way to get out of this bubble is to have recurring, in-depth coffee chats with a friend, family member, or mentor (but you already knew that). It doesn't need to be formal.

In fact, the earliest kernel of this book was planted after the two of us started speaking on the phone every few months during school. These conversations helped us see the unique strengths and weaknesses of our respective schools. They also helped us get tactical feedback on in-the-moment challenges. In short, they helped us take a step back and think about meta-learnings across the MBA experience.

These kinds of quarterly check-ins are also a great way to stay in touch with old friends. Ideally, you'll have a couple of different partners for this activity. Friends from where you grew up, where you went to school, and the workplace will all see and react to your MBA experience with different perspectives. That varied texture is invaluable.

3. Course-based Takeaways

Many of the things you'll learn in business school won't immediately apply to your first job. For example, you may take an in-depth course on leveraged buyout (LBO) modeling, but go into a creative marketing role. But you'll probably run into an LBO-related problem at some point in your career. What then?

Creating a resource full of important takeaways on a topic is a great way to help yourself down the line. In my negotiation class, the final assignment was to write a memo to ourselves five years in the future, when we were about to start a negotiation: things to prepare for, top 10 learnings, resources, etc. It was sort of like a coffee chat between "past me" and "future me." The format is less important than the idea; this can be a memo, set of slides, or simply well-organized file retention. Do whatever will work best for future you.

4. Daily or Weekly Journaling

Things move very fast in business school. Like Ferris Bueller said, blink and you'll miss it. You need a way to make quick course corrections. One of the best ways to keep a pulse on what you're learning is a daily or weekly journal.

You might ask yourself: What do I want to remember about today? When you find your answers redundant or unexciting (you're the judge), you'll know it's time to find a fresh set of activities to continue maximizing the MBA.

THE TAKEAWAY

The point here is not to blindly do the four things above. It's to continue to ask yourself: "How can I maximize my retention and leverage all the information I'm learning?" You can start by picking one or two of the above options and setting up a system before you get to school.

CHAPTER 3

What's the best thing you did in school?

Real Student Answer

"I embraced JOMO [the Joy of Missing Out], which means there was a lot I didn't do. I forced myself to be okay with having the 'right regrets.' As a result, I didn't do clubs, leadership activities, or heavy recruiting. I don't think that's right for everyone, but I do think making some tough choices can be valuable for everyone.

"I also fit most of my schoolwork into the day, which helped me match my partner's schedule a bit more. We were married about two years before school and I was traveling a lot for work. Our relationship was good, but before school we just didn't have that

much quality time together. In school, I prioritized 'us' and our relationship really grew as a result. I don't want to tell Admits to opt out of school activities... that's not my message. But I think you should opt into whatever will allow you to do what's most fulfilling to you. And remember that while these are a 'special two years,' there will always be something in life causing a delay, so just find a way to prioritize NOW, whatever your priorities are."

While the specific responses to this question are unique to everyone, after talking with our friends we realized that there are really just two answers:

1. **The expected stuff.** Often on-campus. Typically from the "standard menu."
2. **The unexpected stuff.** Frequently off-campus. Usually an "off-menu item."

As you might be realizing, we love a good metaphor. Here we continue the food theme, upgrading the MBA from an all-you-can-eat buffet to a really nice, fancy restaurant.

Answer Number 1 is like the restaurant's menu. It's on the table when you arrive and everyone sees it and takes it as the default. There are a ton of options—appetizers, sides, entrees, desserts, drinks, etc.—and they're all great. MBA programs offer a tremendous range of activities and opportunities. Whether it be on-campus recruiting, world-class faculty, interesting clubs, or social events with your classmates, you won't be lacking for options. Most students do a tremendous job of taking advantage of these resources. And at times, a lot of students take advantage of too many of them. It's all part of the journey.

Answer Number 2 is the off-menu choice. It isn't on the table and no one talks about it. You have to ask for it—the chef's specials, the secret speakeasy in the back, the old entrée that was removed but that they'll still make for you if you ask. Fewer students successfully go off-menu. It's easy to miss, especially with so much going on right in front of you. But each year, many students, through their own efforts, uncover unique opportunities that directly relate to their interests. Ultimately, this path less traveled becomes a seminal part of their experience.

Here are four examples of off-menu activities we (or our friends) loved:

1. Auditing an undergraduate class in the engineering school on industrial design sketching: Beyond teaching how to draw, it taught students how to quickly and creatively prototype and communicate ideas—a critical skill when you're in the early stages of launching a business.

2. Starting a photo booth rental company during school and applying all the various learnings from school: The (positive) experience provided a critical feeling of confidence that carried into the post-MBA work world.

3. Participating in a two-day hackathon in downtown Chicago: Working with a local machine-learning engineer and an international database engineer, we built a technical product to solve a real-world problem. It showed the power of a diverse and complementary team.

4. Volunteering extensively (both administratively and in the field) with a local Boys & Girls Club of America: It felt good :).

If the menu comprises activities that are the same every year, off-menu activities are things you pursue specifically for yourself, whether for personal, social, or professional benefit. If you prefer to think less in metaphors, envision these activities as stuff you can literally do off the business school campus. Generally speaking, there are three categories of off-menu opportunities. For each, we've included a couple examples.

1. Atypical Activities That Are Technically On Campus Or Part Of Standard Offerings

- **Different or weird classes.** There is a huge class list within most MBA programs since schools usually allow you to take advantage of their parent institution's courses. Some MBA students take language classes (coding or linguistic) to brush up on their skills, some take an engineering class to build or create things, while others explore law, politics, or some other area of interest.
- **Independent research.** Don't see a class you want? Or want to dig deeper into one you particularly enjoyed? Many schools let you design your own mini-course. With a professor sponsoring your efforts, it can count as credit and double as an opportunity to explore exactly what you want.
- **Going abroad.** Some schools have established study-abroad or international programs. Others have

summer programs with international components. Many students simply do this informally. International students frequently lead trips to their home countries, allowing you to enjoy a trip with classmates while also getting a more intimate look at a different country.

2. Completely Off-campus/Off-menu Activities That Are Related To Your Business School Experience.

- **Working part-time.** Many students work part-time during school, but you'll want to make sure this doesn't affect your financial aid or academics. You may choose to continue your internship from the summer or do something more casual and fun.
- **Starting something new.** Earlier we wrote about the rewards of starting a business during school, but creating a club or group activity might also fire up your creative juices and give you the opportunity to interact with classmates who share your interests.

3. Things Completely Unrelated To Business School. At The End Of The Day, We're All Just Normal People, But That's Often Forgotten In The B-school Bubble.

- **Volunteering.** Most schools are in highly populated areas with tons of programs, organizations, and opportunities to give back.
- **City-league sports.** The concentration of young alumni around schools often makes for a robust intramural sports scene. Chances are you'll be able to find pickup

games with your classmates pretty often, but joining a local league is a great way to play even more and meet some locals.

- **Informally coordinating.** This can be a habit more than an overarching thing. There's an entire world out there to explore, with or without B-school classmates. Organize dinners. Pursue a hobby. Find unique activities.

THE TAKEAWAY

Once you're on campus, it's easy to forget about the off-menu. Don't. Finding something 100 percent authentic to your interests, even if you have to blaze a path, is a foolproof way to make the most of your time. Make a list right now of some activities you'd like to pursue and leave a reminder to yourself to revisit it at the beginning of every quarter. Far be it for us to recommend something that applies to your life, but know that going off-menu was one of the most fulfilling aspects of our MBA experience. We highly recommend it.

CHAPTER 4

What does a week look like?

Real Student Answer

"I don't know. It feels like they all were different. During the first few weeks, I literally can't remember what happened. Then during recruiting it felt like I was constantly switching into professional clothes for interviews or information sessions. I guess outside of that, my most general week was probably being on campus from roughly 9:00–3:00, including both class and homework. I'd often then work out or do something active for a couple hours before going home and grabbing dinner (sometimes with roommates). If I had to, I'd do more work, otherwise I'd get ready for whatever social event there was. Probably once a month I'd travel for at least a weekend, too, which would then often

mean the week was busier as I fit in all of my chores and whatever work I didn't get done over the weekend."

This is a super-tactical question (good job, question-asker!) yet so hard to answer since it varies so much between people. Every week can be so different. Early days vs. steady state. Recruiting or not. First year or second year. Coupled, single, or with kids. Heavy involvement in clubs. And so on.

That being the case, the best response may be to give you some data and let you come to your own conclusions. Just below we've screenshotted two calendar snapshots from two different former MBA students. We've cleansed the images for privacy and to make them easier to read, but the raw information should be illuminating. We'll let you know what we think. But first you should come to your own conclusions.

Before we dive in, some context: The first screenshot is from an MBA1 with a fairly social calendar. The second is from an MBA2 with a more relaxed (or less scheduled) social life:

Mon 9	Tue 10	Wed 11	Thu 12	Fri 13
	FRIENDS			
		WORKOUT W/ FRIEND		SLEEP IN
CLASS: OPERATNS		CAREER EVENT		CLASS: OPERATNS
LUNCH W/ FRIEND	GUEST SPEAKER	STUDENT GVNMT LUNCH		
CLASS: ACCNTG	CLASS: CORP FINANCE		CLASS: CORP FINANCE	CLASS: ACCNTNG
CLASS: CAPITAL MARKETS	CLASS: INTERPERS DYNAMICS		CLASS: LEADERSHIP COACHING	CLASS: CAPITAL MARKETS
APARTMNT HUNTING				WEEKEND FLIGHT
	SECTION HAPPY HOUR			
	CLASS: INTERPERS DYNAMICS	SCHOOL SOCIAL		
		WEEKLY CLASSMATE TALK		
	SOCIAL		WEEKLY BAR EVENT	

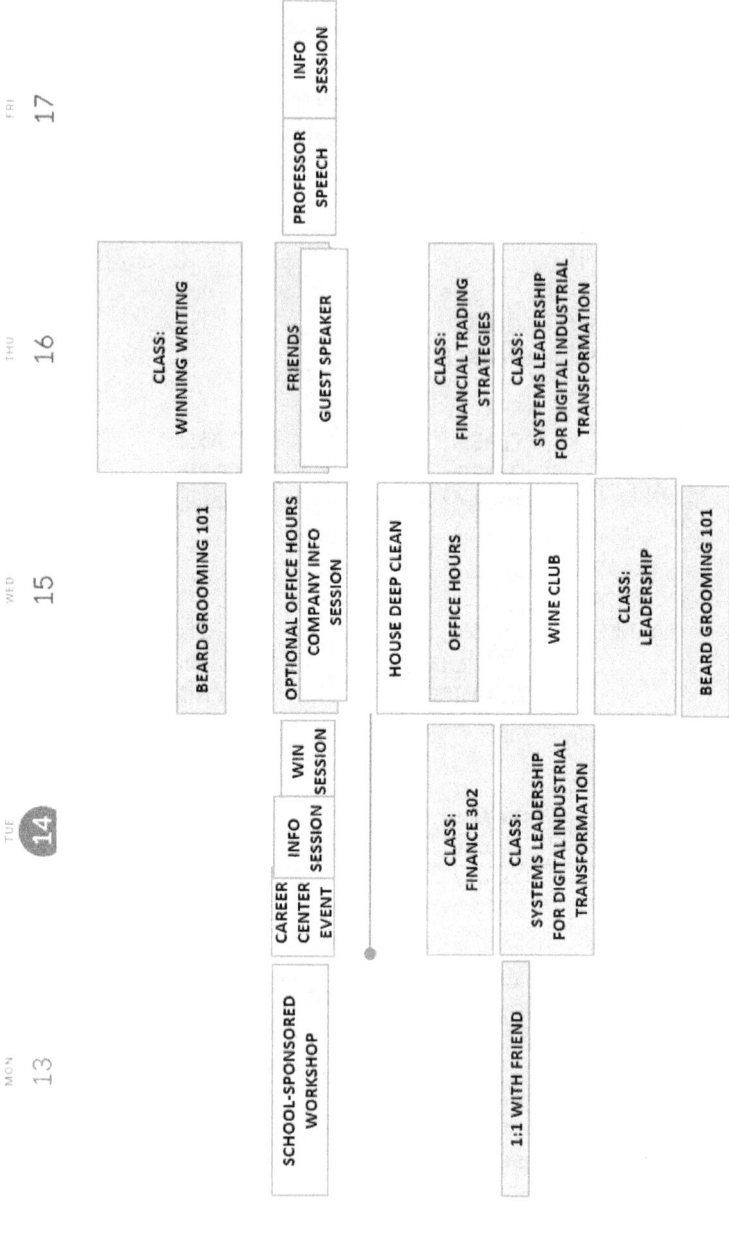

While the calendars differ quite a bit, they reveal certain universal truths about every MBA experience. Here are six.

1. Generally, You Have A Lot Of Time—but It Disappears Fast.

People talk about how busy business school is. But both calendars have significant gaps in various places. How can you be busy and have a lot of time? Well, for a couple of reasons. First, students have less flexibility than people in the work world. You can't take PTO to skip a week of class. And while you have far more free time versus working full time, you will have far more options competing for your attention. You have a greater supply of time, but also way more demand for it.

2. Class Schedules Vary Wildly.

If you look at MBA2's calendar, you'll notice a lot more free time. They are probably coasting towards graduation with a lighter class load—potentially using their extra time to focus on an off-menu item. Over the course of your two years, it's common to adjust your workload as needed and prioritize when you have class.

Conversely, MBA1 has a more traditional class schedule. This makes it tougher to travel. Tragically, this person had to wait until after Friday classes before flying out for a music festival. The horror! However, they've avoided having any class before 10 a.m. Nice.

3. Social Calendars Can Be Nonstop.

MBA1's calendar is a good representation of the amount of activity in a socially active student's life. Looking at the bottom of the calendar, you can see weekly social events on Tuesday,

Wednesday, and Thursday, as well as several other one-off events. Furthermore, MBA1 has a Friday flight out to a music festival that weekend, and from experience we know that just about everything will repeat next week.

All of which is to say: If you're an extrovert, get ready for a ton of fun over the next two years. Few environments offer the same combination of affluence, creativity, and enthusiasm for social gatherings like business school.

If you're an introvert or this sounds like a bit much, fret not. Not everyone takes part in all of these activities. In fact, few people consistently attend everything. As always, it's all about your priorities. But know that a strong social scene will likely be available at your school and that some of your classmates will be taking advantage of everything, or at least trying to. If you're not going to be in that group, just remember you can always take solace in JOMO: the Joy of Missing Out.

4. Random Stuff Is Always Happening.

There are lots of weekly activities. But there are always one-off things popping up, too. Examples in these calendars include "Madden Draft" and "Beard Grooming 101." We've even seen a calendar that had 60 minutes blocked out to "Find a rabbit." Invariably, you'll always have something weird going on. For many people, this is one of the best parts about school.

5. There Are Lots Of Organized Sessions.

Especially in MBA2's calendar, you'll notice lots of activities in the "Other" category around lunchtime. These are all official activities organized through the school. As you'll soon discover, they span a wide range, from recruiting meet-and-greets to affinity group conversations to hot topic presentations and even simple "brown bag lunches." Many "Other" activities are completely random and hard to codify. There are often several things happening at once, and you'll have to make countless decisions of what to do throughout your MBA, choosing from many things that won't happen again.

6. There Is An Invisible But Significant Amount Of Calendar "Dark Matter."

One thing that's not reflected in the calendars is time spent outside the classroom on academics. For certain classes, and depending on your strengths as a student, this may take up a huge chunk of time. Many experiential learning classes may also have significant out-of-classroom commitments. Some students also simply require more time to keep up academically. Perhaps school will be easy for you (or you'll choose not to invest the time in it), but this academic "dark matter" takes up a lot of time for many MBA students.

THE TAKEAWAY

Perhaps the best way to understand the basics of the MBA experience is to just see what it looks like. If this calendar concept seems interesting but you want a resource that's more relevant to your school (and thus your life), here's a great question to ask in coffee chats: "Would you mind sharing a screenshot of your calendar during X?" The "X" can be recruiting, the first few weeks of school, or any other period of interest to you.

PART 2

THE TOP THREE
CONCERNS

CHAPTER 5

How can I maintain a strong relationship with my partner?

Real Student Answer

"This was just a matter of priorities. My partner was a priority over school and that made it easy. I think if someone has a different set of priorities, communication becomes super important. There's nothing wrong with that, and in fact a lot of people decide to go all in on school for two years. Often their partners join them socially. But it becomes important to stay on the same page so resentment doesn't build while the relationship itself plays second fiddle."

When we recently googled "being in a relationship MBA," three of the first four related search terms were "MBA relationship killer," "MBA marriage breaker," and "MBA divorce." Yikes.

Not everybody enters school coupled, but many do and have (including us). Maintaining a strong relationship with your partner during an MBA can be hard. But the good news is there are lots of ways you can make it easier.

Before we offer some tips, though, let's dig into why these relationships can be hard...

1. Different Contexts

When you start your MBA, you enter a crazy new world and your day-to-day life suddenly becomes completely different. Your partner is probably still working, though. Their average day is pretty close to what it was like beforehand. But your life has changed in nearly every dimension. You're meeting hundreds of new people, trying hundreds of new things, and likely changing in hundreds of ways. This drastic context differential can cause couples to grow apart.

2. Misaligned Schedules

You may be free from 12:00–4:00 p.m. and busy all night while they're on a typical 9:00–5:00 schedule. This can make it significantly harder to find time together, much less quality time.

3. FOMO

You can easily seesaw between feeling selfish and despairing from the fear of missing out (FOMO). When you go to events, you feel like you're leaving your partner behind. When you skip the event for date night, you feel like you're not capitalizing on the investment you're making.

4. Big Decisions

At this stage in your life, you'll have to confront multiple big, ambiguous decisions that affect you both, and all at once. What type of jobs should you pursue? What cities should you pursue them in? How do these career choices affect your family plans? Should you prioritize one of your careers over the other? There's no easy or direct way to answer these questions, and it can be particularly hard to find an answer together.

5. Money

One of you will be spending it and one of you will be making it. It's easy for resentment to build—especially when so many "events" seem like happy hours.

6. False Expectations

Few of us come into the MBA experience fully aware of how hard maintaining our romantic relationships can be. Very few schools and students talk about the challenges openly, and it shocks many couples when they first start experiencing them (particularly when it comes to list items #1 and #2).

This may seem terrible, but even just acknowledging these struggles is half the battle. One tactical thing you can do right now: discuss the issues touched on just above with your partner. You can do this! For what it's worth, we're both happily married to the partners we had through MBA school. In fact, overall, our MBA time was very positive for our relationships.

Relationships are unique and everyone will give you different advice.

Here's the advice (in summary form) nearly all of our friends recommended...

1. Decide On Your Partner's Involvement Early On.

If they want to, get them involved socially at the very beginning. Lots of couples end up waiting a month or two, and then the non-student feels like they don't belong. Bring them to everything you can and get them added to Slack or whatever you use ASAP. Or if that's not what you/your partner wants, then actively say no. The point is to make that decision very early.

2. Block Out Time On Your Calendar For You To Be Together.

"I'm their fifth class", we heard from one person speaking for exasperated partners of grad students everywhere. Despite their obvious frustration, there's some helpful instruction here, too. Whether it's something active (cooking) or passive (watching a movie), instituting some sort of ritual or routine that is ironclad and non-cancelable was suggested by nearly everyone.

3. Over-communicate Your Goals And Needs.

And ask your partner to do the same. Don't assume they can read your mind when you say stuff like "I'm going to a happy hour." Tell them about the company hosting it and how excited you are about the chance for a summer internship with them.

4. Share Your Calendar Proactively And Often.

This is especially important when it comes to big events that you'd like your partner to attend.

And here's some additional advice that a few people hyper-passionately recommended...

1. Bring Your Work Structure Home.

This might feel cringey, but bring some professionalism and order into your relationship: feedback meetings every week, weekend vacations to design a family culture, Excel for trip planning, etc. Anything to create predictability and control in an out-of-control environment.

2. Two Words: Couples Therapy.

A surprisingly high number of people we surveyed did proactive couples therapy during school to get ahead of any potential issues.

3. Go All In.

Don't treat this time as something temporary that you "just get through." Invest in your MBA community together and really work on things as they come up. It's too easy to write off these two years of your life as just a stop on the way to someplace else.

On the other hand, the quickest way to ensure you do *not* maximize your time at school is to de-prioritize the person most important to you. With a little planning and honest communication, this can be an amazing time for you both.

THE TAKEAWAY

Maintaining your relationships during school can be challenging, primarily because the experience demands so much of your time and energy. But every year hundreds of MBA students and their partners succeed in maintaining, and often strengthening, their bond. It starts with setting expectations appropriately, and requires ongoing intentional decisions, some tactical coordination and, of course, the desire to work through things together.

CHAPTER 6

How should I prioritize my time?

Real Student Answer

"There's so much groupthink on prioritization that I think it can be easy to just listen to what everyone else says. But what are your priorities? I'd ask yourself that first and then use that to inform the choices you make. It's easy to stray from those priorities, so this takes a degree of discipline. Just know that you'll have to say NO to something."

This question sometimes surfaces in a more specific way, as in, "Should I do XYZ? Is it worth it?" Either way, the answer is a bit counterintuitive.

All of our friends who loved and valued the MBA the most had one thing in common: they were very clear about what they were NOT interested in. You're going to have enough activities to fill 1,000 percent of your time. So it's important for you to cut out vast categories of options and make quick decisions. Success won't just come from finding your passion or choosing what to do. It's just as important to find your anti-passions: the things you definitely don't want to do.

We're not saying that you should be closed off, just that there are too many resources out there to be open to everything. The people that struggle the most are the ones that say yes to everything. They end up dabbling and never diving deep.

During our frequent talks, we often reminded each other that JOMO > FOMO. Saying no frees up time, keeps you healthy, and forces focus. Think especially carefully about signing up for long-term, non-reversible decisions in your first quarter. Things like a two-year fellowship or one-year club leadership role may sound amazing at first, but your interests may drastically change over time.

It's also worth noting that one of the most important things you'll build during this time in your life is a healthy network of smart, ambitious friends that like and trust you. The most common way people burn that trust is by signing up for too much and then dropping an activity last minute or delivering poor work. You don't want to be that person.

Consistently saying "no" can feel a little weird at first. One tactic is to start by making a list of the activities, industries, and jobs you definitely don't care about. Maybe you're coming from banking and know that you're not interested in going back. And maybe you're a military vet and are already confident in your leadership skills. You might have a list that says, "I won't go to banking recruiting events and I won't volunteer to lead clubs." This way, when banking recruiting kicks off in four months and half the school is talking about it, you won't feel tempted.

This strategy doesn't just apply to career and personal development. You can use it to prioritize across your academics, social life, health, career, and more. For example, one of our friends made a rule for one quarter that he wouldn't go to any social event with over ten people on the invite list. He wanted to focus on going deeper with a smaller set of friends. He found that physically writing down the rule made it easier to follow through on.

This brings up a subtle point: your list isn't static. You should make an initial list before you get to school, but know that it will change as you change. You'll find an ebb and flow to your prioritization. Some activities will feel more or less important over time while others will be mainstays.

THE TAKEAWAY

As awkward as it may feel, take the time to create a list of priorities and "depriorities"—things you will say no to. Doing this in advance makes it easier to make snap decisions that align with your personal MBA goals.

CHAPTER 7

How can I grow and get better?

Real Student Answer

"Before school, I was used to getting consistent feedback at work. Sometimes I had a boss that did it in a structured way, and other times I had to claw it out of them, but either way feedback was always important to my growth and general self-awareness. But at school it was a bit different. Everyone's trying so hard to make friends that it sometimes feels impossible to get real feedback or understanding. Near the end I had some great heart-to-hearts with some friends and it was immensely valuable. I wish I had done that more."

One of the best and most unique things we did during school was take an intentional and consistent approach to getting peer feedback. It was a catalyst for self-reflection, growth, and friendship.

Similar to note-taking and portfolio building, there are multiple ways you can go about gaining peer feedback. Pick what's best for you and adapt it to what works. The important thing is to just do something—anything is better than nothing.

Start by keeping it very simple. After every group project, pick one or two teammates and ask if they'd be open to exchanging feedback. It'll feel awkward at first. Push past that.

If they agree (and they always will), take the first step and send them an email with two strengths and two potential things they could do differently. Keep it relatively short with three to five sentences (max) for each point and a specific example. Then ask them to do the same for you.

You'll get helpful feedback in return most of the time. Sometimes it'll reveal an annoying habit or weakness you haven't considered. Sometimes it'll highlight a strength you didn't even realize you had. Regardless, it will make you a more empathetic teammate and a better creator.

It's worth experimenting with in-person feedback vs email. They each have pros and cons. The great thing about email is that you'll have a record of your strengths and weaknesses that you can return to in the future if you want to measure your progress. Email also gives the feedback provider time to better structure their thoughts.

The best thing about in-person is that it's a bonding experience. You'd be surprised how many close relationships start with a deep heart-to-heart over feedback. In-person feedback also usually leads to more direct and honest feedback because the feedback giver won't be worried about leaving a paper trail or not being able to explain themselves if there's a misunderstanding.

Ok, so you're convinced and doing feedback after every project. What comes next?

Eventually it will stop feeling awkward. At that point you can begin asking for much more frequent feedback and much more in-depth feedback.

Give a speech in class? Ask the person next to you for feedback as soon as you sit back down. Get into an argument during a group project? Ask someone else on the team how you handled it.

You can even push this one step further and start asking people for ongoing, always-on feedback. For example, if you'd like to work on not saying 'um' as much, you might ask a close friend to continuously give you feedback on it. It's often the fastest way to improve.

Beyond professional skills, you can use feedback to understand the impact and impression you're making on people. How do you show up?

During my last academic quarter, I had an intense group project with five close friends. Everyone was very comfortable with feedback and decided to push it even further. We scheduled time together and each answered three questions about everyone else in the group. (1) What could they do better? (2) What do they do really well? (3) What was your first impression of them and how has it changed over time?

We then got drinks and went around and shared the answers. It was awesome. There was so much love, friendly challenge, and growth.

As illuminating as the first two questions were, the third one was the secret sauce.

Do you know what type of impact you make on people when you meet them? Probably not. Even worse, it's way too awkward to ask just anyone about this. But your friends will remember. And that's priceless information. Maybe you're coming across as quiet when you want to be charismatic. Maybe you come across as a jerk. There's only one way to find out.

It goes without saying, but this is also great leadership training. You're probably going to be leading a team soon. This allows you to get comfortable giving and getting feedback if you aren't already.

Some people will read this and say, "Of course I'll do that. I already do that." Great! Keep it up. The rest of you will say, "Lol, that sounds so ridiculous." Maybe. But why not give it a chance? It's one of the most high-value things you can do. It's also way weirder and way harder to do outside of business school, so if you're going to make a fool out of yourself, you might as well do it now.

THE TAKEAWAY

Gather peer feedback throughout the MBA experience. It will probably feel awkward but that's okay. Choose the method that feels most natural to you and zealously pursue it.

PART 3

THE TACTICAL STUFF

CHAPTER 8

Should I get a club leadership role?

Real Student Answer

"I avoided this like the plague. Clubs can be fantastically helpful and a great way to find your crew. But leading them always seemed like unpaid labor to me (because it is). I had other things that I thought were more important and that I wanted to spend time on. That said, most of my friends disagreed with me and found them fun and valuable. Particularly those that were pivoting careers."

Being a leader in a club can be fulfilling. But we think people too often jump in blindly without really considering their goals. Remember, business school is fundamentally an opportunity cost/zero-sum game. Everything you do prevents you from doing something else. Some of our friends had really good reasons for getting a club leadership role. Others had terrible reasons. Let's talk about both.

We'll begin by exploring why being a club leader might *not* be a good idea. When you ask people why they want to lead a club, you hear three major reasons: it's a résumé booster, it's a leadership opportunity, and it won't take up that much time. In most cases, these reasons aren't actually true. Here's why.

1. Most Companies Don't Really Care That You Were The Tech Club Treasurer.

A leadership position may seem like an important résumé differentiator, but it often isn't. Keep in mind that most recruiters and managers were also an MBA and often in club leadership roles. They know that many of these roles don't equate to job readiness. And that lots of people—quite possibly themselves—signed on just to beef up their résumé.

2. It Might Not Actually Give You Leadership Experience.

Most clubs don't offer real leadership opportunities. You're "leading" five other peers that are also "leading" you. Clubs aren't designed to be efficient. They are designed to be inclusive and to spread work across as many people as possible. Meanwhile, there are no real positive or negative incentives to do quality work. This combo leads to a maximum number of roles and a minimum amount of real management or leadership experience.

3. It Might Take Up Too Much Time.

Lots of people involved = lots of meetings. Most club leadership roles end up taking a lot of time. There are planning meetings, actual work to be done, and of course, the events your club is putting on. You'd be shocked at how much time it takes to put on a good event! Overall, being in a leadership position takes up a lot of time without necessarily providing any benefits that a regular member won't also receive. Plus, a lot of your work is administrative. You might get bored.

Despite these challenges, there are good reasons to lead a club.

1. It May Be A Great Way To Build Alumni And Career Relationships.

Everyone wants to be the president of the club. But there's another leadership role that is secretly amazing: the "alumni" and/or "speaker" role. This person is usually in charge of bringing in interesting people to speak to the club. This role allows you to build valuable connections with people you'd want to network with anyhow. Instead of cold emailing that Google Product Manager, you can email them about coming in to speak to the club. And then, once you've built up a rapport, that's when you ambush them. (Just kidding. Sort of.) It's a great way to complement your recruiting strategy.

2. It May Be A Great Way To Build Peer Relationships.

Business school is all about relationship building. The best way to get to know someone is to work with them. Joining a club leadership team is an easy way to get to know a small group of people with similar interests on a deeper level. If you think the leadership team of a particular club is fun or cool or smart, then yeah, join it. You'll get to know them really well.

3. It May Be Really Fun.

This is probably the best reason to take on a leadership role. Kellogg had a BBQ club. If you love BBQ, then forget about everything we just said. Join the leadership team and you'll have a great excuse to spend time doing something you love.

4. To give back to a community that helped you.

Student leadership is the engine that drives most MBA programs. If nobody took on club leadership roles, the MBA experience would be less effective in a variety of ways. Leading a club is a great way to contribute to your school and can be very fulfilling. For example, if you're a second year and the Consulting Club is the number-one reason you got that fancy job at McKinsey, then you might want to pay it forward by taking on a leadership role and helping those coming up behind you.

A quick caveat. There are two specific situations where our "terrible reasons to join a club" don't apply. First, if you're coming from a non-feeder/unorthodox background and trying to break into a new career, then a related club can be good for your résumé. Second, you can get real leadership experience if you're the president of a large club with real responsibility (e.g., running a 300-person two-day health care conference with a five-person team).

THE TAKEAWAY

There are some good reasons to pursue a club leadership role, but also plenty of reasons to deprioritize this part of the experience. Either way, it should be a relatively low-stakes decision. It won't make or break your time at business school. No need to stress.

CHAPTER 9

When should I quit my pre-MBA job?

Real Student Answer

"I had saved up a decent amount of money at the time and was also lucky to be living with my partner, who had a great job and was willing to support me. Given that cushy scenario, I quit pretty early and used the time to prepare for school, decompress from working 100+ hour weeks for years, and have some fun."

The answer to this question is a budgeting exercise. You want to make sure you are financially ready to trade income for independence.

Many alumni will tell you to quit immediately. They'll reminisce on their months before business school, wistfully recounting travel, relaxation, and happiness. It's certainly an attractive possibility.

But you need enough access to cash (savings, loans, sponsorship, etc.) to be happy through school. If you're not there yet, working a few extra months to build up your savings will help you make the most of your time in school.

There's no need to over-model this. As you'll learn in accounting, simply understand your sources of cash and compare them against your uses of cash. Anything else is probably false precision.

Let's start with those sources of cash.

1. How Much Do You Have Now?

Specifically, assets you will use for school. This pool should not include your retirement funds or anything else you do not want to touch. Maybe you're willing to dip into an IRA or emergency fund; we'll let you define what falls within a 'no fly' zone and what's available for use. Just decide in advance.

2. How Much Will You Earn During The Next Two Years When You're A Student?

Many people assume they will have zero income for two years. That might be the case, but it also doesn't have to be true. Depending on when you quit your pre-MBA job and start your post-MBA job, you can start to squeeze that timeline. You can also generate income from full-time internships, part-time jobs, liquidating assets, merit-based aid, relocation and signing bonuses. All of this can be used to cover living expenses and/or help with tuition.

3. How Much Aid Will You Receive?

Schools have a mathematical formula to calculate the amount of aid applicants are eligible for. Most schools provide access to their financial aid office and explain roughly how the formula works. You've likely already heard what your aid package is, but if not, feel free to reach out to your school for some guidelines. For example, many schools provide need-based aid based on assets, not income. So if you've saved aggressively, you might not get aid. That said, all schools are different.

Note that being married will likely lower your aid package. If you're single—at least from an IRS standpoint—you'll probably have fewer assets and less income during school. This certainly shouldn't drive your personal decision-making, but make sure you know the implications should you decide to get married during school.

4. How Much Debt Do You Need?

In the end, many people need substantial loans. Even if you don't absolutely need to, you may want to consider financing your MBA instead of using savings to pay for it. Post-school refinancing rates for high earners with job security can be exceptionally low. Obviously, this will change based on the interest rate environment, so check this out for yourself.

We considered providing details here about specific debt financing options, but these often change or become outdated. Ask a professional for in-depth advice, but also know that your classmates will be an amazing resource to you. Someone in your class will inevitably be a personal finance guru who has put in hours of work to find the best rates. In our experience, they are happy to share this knowledge.

Now for the uses of cash—aka school and living expenses.

1. Start With The "Total Cost Of Attendance."

Most schools publish these figures online. Just google your school and "total cost of attendance." While the expense categories are broad, they offer a good starting point for most of your expected expenses.

However, many students change their lifestyle during school. If you're planning to have kids or get a dog, you'll want to consider that. Furthermore, school-provided health care is not the most cost-effective option. It may offer incredibly high-quality care and be a wonderfully convenient option, but that may not matter to you. Make sure you shop around to find competitive rates and coverage options.

2. Add A Substantial Buffer.

The school-released "total cost of attendance" figures are generally very conservative. Most MBAs do not live the 'moderate lifestyle' that these schools refer to. For example, many international trips cost more than $3,000. MBAs often take two or three per year plus several weekend trips. And many MBAs enjoy living in nice apartments or group houses. The magnitude of these expenses isn't always accounted for in the schools' estimates. Depending on how you live, consider a healthy buffer of 10 to 20 percent or more.

Ultimately, it's up to you how rigorously you want to prepare. One option is to add all of this information into a detailed cash flow model (there are lots of them online) that adjusts for loans and lifestyle and use that information to decide when to quit. Another is to play it a little bit looser. You probably have a good, intuitive idea of your budget and needs, and there's no reason to over-model it as long as you continue to check and adapt each semester.

THE TAKEAWAY

Quitting your job as soon as possible is an exciting idea—especially after years of hard work. But don't underestimate the planning required to ensure your peace of mind. We've both heard from regretful students who quit too soon and felt like they couldn't do certain trips and expensive activities during school for budget reasons. Don't let poor budgeting affect your MBA experience. Keep it simple. Be conservative. But do some financial planning.

CHAPTER 10

How do I find a pre-MBA internship (if I want one)?

Real Student Answer

"This exercise was all about prioritization and discipline. I knew I wasn't going to find something perfect, so I focused on finding something good enough. I made a list of companies and just grinded. It paid off and the extra experience was helpful for figuring out what I wanted to do next. And it looked great on my résumé."

There are lots of people who just want to travel or relax before school and not work. If that's you, cool—enjoy doing you. And while you're at it, feel free to skip ahead. We're not going to waste your time telling you how to enjoy yourself.

But if you're not sure what you want to do before school starts, we'd encourage you to consider a pre-MBA internship. Presuming you're able to quit early enough and/or land a well-paying gig, it can provide a delightful combination of fiscal responsibility and relaxation.

It's often a nice way to decelerate into school with a change of scenery and continued income. It also allows you to test out a new career and potentially get a leg up for your summer internship recruiting by helping you better understand your interests. If it doesn't work out, you've ruled out one more path—and still have the summer between Year 1 and Year 2 to test another career with your internship.

We've heard many Admits and anonymous online usernames suggest that landing an internship before Year 1 is impossible. We disagree (and have the proof—we did it!). It will likely take a fair amount of outreach, but it's definitely possible to find a good pre-MBA internship.

To that end, here are some tips for landing an internship before school. All of them are based on personal and peer experiences.

1. Be Deliberate.

We recommend starting your search as soon as possible. It may go quickly, but it also can take several months to find something. You want to leave plenty of time for the internship and a few weeks off after that. If an internship is important to you, be super conservative with your planning. Budget two months for searching, four to six months for interning, and one month to relax. If you find something quickly, just do a longer "internship." From an employer's perspective, longer is usually an easier sell anyway.

Make a tracker in Excel/Google Sheets. If you're doing this right, it'll be hard to keep track of everywhere you reach out, their contact information, and how you found them. Some people will respond weeks later and you won't remember the original context.

Lastly, check if your school has a program to help with internship placement. Some might even provide funding for you to work at nonprofits or early-stage startups. The easiest path would be your school placing you in an existing opportunity.

2. Know One Thing You Want.

This might be obvious, but it's really helpful to know what you want to get out of the experience before you start. Do you want to test a career path? Develop a skill? Add to your résumé for recruiting? There are countless reasons. Know yours, but don't have too many. You want a north star, but you don't want to have such a lengthy wish list that it disqualifies good-enough options and thus lowers your chance of success.

3. Know One (Or Three) Thing(s) You Can Give.

We're all nice, eager, and hard-working, but these traditional intern traits probably won't cut it this time. Fortunately, if you've been admitted to a full-time MBA program you probably have years of experience and valuable skills. If those skills are relevant to a company, you'll dramatically increase your odds of getting hired. It's hard to know their exact needs, but share your skills and hope for a match. Your experience will not only help them infer your abilities but also communicate your value succinctly. For example, you can keep your first email much shorter by saying you were a management consultant for three years (instead of saying that you are analytical, detail-oriented, and an excellent communicator). Whatever your experience, use it to help illustrate your abilities. If your experience is relevant, most people can deduce your long list of skills.

4. Determine Your Price.

If you're successful, the company you're applying to will eventually ask for your rate or comp. It's easy to forget to prepare for this, but have an answer in mind. Obviously, your price is personal. If you find the experience you're about to have valuable and rare, you may want to accept less compensation if that's what's offered. One approach is to maintain your school savings rate. However, you may also factor in things like halting your 401k contributions, living with family to save rent, and shortening your commute. That could all factor into your ask.

5. Hustle For Warm Intros.

Like all networking, a warm intro is far more effective than a cold outreach. So be creative: Who do you know that might want a "pretern"? Or who could connect you with people like that? Former managers or colleagues with an MBA might be able to introduce you to their old classmates. And don't forget about those managers or colleagues who have moved on to interesting companies. If you worked at an investment firm, your portfolio companies could be great options; then again, a childhood basketball teammate's parents' local business might be fun. In our experience, someone who would hire a pretern is likely to value your skill set, be familiar with MBAs, and work at a small/growing company. Alumni of your MBA program are probably willing to help with your search; they are often extremely eager to talk to incoming students. Almost everyone uniquely finds their company, but most had an element of the warm intro. And everybody hustled.

6. Prioritize Brevity Over Completeness In Your Emails.

This may seem obvious, but we'll spell it out anyway: If the person you'd like to hire you has a need that matches your skills, they'll follow up for more info. If they don't, then no amount of selling will open that door. It just won't. Here is an example of a cold outreach note:

> Hello X, I've been following Kimpossible for years and am hoping to work with you this summer. I have three years' consulting experience at Y and am heading to Chico State in the fall. I'm looking for a pre-school internship to use my software skills while I learn about mission planning. If there might be an opportunity to join you, I'd love to schedule 20 minutes to talk more...

Short and sweet. Just enough to hook them. Note that it also builds on what we said above: know one thing you want and one thing you can give.

7. Don't Make Things Harder Than They Have To Be.

This is abnormal recruiting. Which means it involves extra work for whoever's hiring you. Minimize that as much as possible and you'll increase your chances. Stick to countries where you are authorized to work already. Generally, look for local opportunities to avoid moving logistics. Find or create roles that make sense for you and the company.

8. Small Companies Have The Largest Odds.

Large companies have formal hiring processes, start dates, and target profiles. A pre-MBA doesn't fit that mold. Your best bets are startups and other small, private companies. This can include investment firms, local businesses, venture-backed startups, PE-backed businesses, and probably a few other types. Avoid red tape and home in on decision makers.

9. Take A Portfolio Approach.

Ultimately, you'll probably get more non-responses than rejections, and more rejections than interest. For example, we probably reached out to twenty-five companies and had various 'interviews' with four; it was impossible to predict which would respond and even harder to know which would hit. One of our interviews came through a former manager and felt promising. Another came through an online application for interns (a signal the company was definitely hiring). The fourth company went from intro to handshake in two weeks, rather unexpectedly.

THE TAKEAWAY

There are tons of good reasons to do an internship before business school, and plenty of opportunities to do so. While this path may not be for everyone, if you choose to pursue it, you'll have to work hard to land an offer. Few companies (if any) are targeting incoming MBA interns, so you'll have to convince people why you're valuable to them.

CHAPTER 11

How can I figure out what job I want?

Real Student Answer

"I felt SO lost when I started business school. Even worse, I felt a little embarrassed that I didn't know. So many of my friends had clear plans while I had no clue. In hindsight, I overreacted. School allowed me to experiment with so many different things, and I eventually found what was right for me."

If you already know exactly what you want to do, feel free to skip this section. However, we've found that most Admits are at least a little unsure. They may have a career in mind, but usually also some doubts up through and even after graduation. Thus, most coffee chats touch on career exploration.

Most of us come into school overexposed to the popular career options: consulting, finance, or whatever our school's popular path is. It creates a self-fulfilling prophecy. Because we know so much about these popular choices, we're more likely to pursue them. Then we return to recruit new students, and the cycle repeats.

Before school and in the first handful of weeks, we recommend expanding the range of careers you'd consider. This will either help confirm your current hypotheses or introduce you to an awesome new option.

Everyone will agree that prioritization is important. But prioritizing too early can be as dangerous as prioritizing too late. When you arrive at school, you'll have access to a new and vast pool of resources. You should take advantage of them to truly understand all the opportunities available to you. Fortunately, this usually requires only a minimal effort.

We recommend taking a 'trial-and-error' approach, or test and learn. You can start with simple tests, like doing internet research, reviewing social media threads on the topic, or talking to someone in the industry. If a career seems interesting, you can deploy bigger tests. These might include taking a class, working part time, or an internship.

This testing process should continue throughout your MBA until you've decided on a career. When school begins, we recommend starting broadly. In the first few weeks, add to your list as you hear of new areas of interest, but also remove things as you go.

But let's backtrack and talk about what you can do before you even step foot on campus. Here are three low-effort ways you can start exploring job options.

1. If You Haven't Already, Check Out Your School's Employment Report.

The level of detail will vary from school to school, but seeing some stats should force you to consider the full range of potential options. Most reports will have a breakdown by industry and function with either a number or percentage of students pursuing those paths. Pay just as much attention to the less popular ones. They're revealing in two ways. First, they show you that other people have already successfully pursued them. It's a beaten path you can follow! You won't have to start from scratch and you know the industry is open to hiring MBAs. Second, there is far more variety across these roles which, purely by statistics, increases the chance that at least one is a great fit for you. To be clear, we're not advocating you choose these careers. We're advocating that you learn about them.

2. Do The Basic Internet Research. Adding Community Tags Like 'reddit' Or 'quora' To Your Search Queries Can Be A Great Way To Get Informal Perspectives.

Try to expose yourself to the basic pros and cons of the industries you're researching. Do they resonate with you? Does the opportunity to work alone excite you because of the independence it offers, or will a lack of teammates depress you? Are you qualified for these jobs? Answer some of the basics and note which questions you still have.

3. Get Coffee With Alumni Or Students You Know From An Industry Or Space You're Interested In Learning About.

If you go this route, you should clarify that you're not recruiting at that moment. Especially in competitive fields like consulting, people may be wary of you reaching out for information, instead of viewing it as an attempt to get a leg up. But almost everyone is happy to offer perspective and answer questions about their experience. Furthermore, alumni from less-well-traveled paths are often especially excited to speak with students about what they know. They haven't been barraged with requests like many of their peers in more traditional fields. Not only can you ask them about their career, but you can also ask them about their school experience. That way, even if the career is ultimately uninteresting to you, the conversation was still valuable.

You may want to prioritize less popular fields, mainly because they're harder to explore on your own. The most popular jobs will have tons of information available during on-campus recruiting; it won't be hard to learn about them. With the limited time you have, your best use of time is learning about the options you don't already know of.

Once you show up at school, you can continue this intelligence-gathering process. You'll now be able to talk with your classmates and any lecturers who are also practitioners with some degree of baseline knowledge. Hopefully, this will help you focus on one of a couple options. Then companies will start coming to campus and providing even more information. Career centers can help make you aware of all the various sources of information. As you start to home in on a primary hypothesis, you can then consider working part-time and recruiting for an internship in your now deliberately chosen field. With each of these escalating steps, you're testing different options. Eventually you'll be exactly where you want to be.

THE TAKEAWAY

Your MBA program will provide tons of career exploration resources that you didn't have prior to school. Unless you're 100 percent positive of your career path, take advantage of these new resources to explore new and diverse potential career paths. Find ways to quickly test and eliminate fields in order to prioritize your time on the careers that excite you most.

CHAPTER 12

Should I start a business?

Real Student Answer

"Starting a business in school was the best thing I did. It's been two years since I graduated and I still leverage the contacts, money, and skills from that experience nearly every day. It literally changed my life."

At the beginning of this book, we said that one of the most important questions you should ask yourself early in your MBA experience is: How can I retain as much information as possible? Well, one powerful way is to apply your learning to a project. This could take the form of case competitions, in-quarter internships, or even a personal blog. But the project I'd recommend the most is starting a business. It doesn't get any more real-life than throwing all of your amazing ideas at the mercies of the market.

We're both very biased. We each started a business our second year and had deeply meaningful experiences. Further, several of our best friends did the same throughout school, and one of our biggest regrets is not starting earlier.

Obvious caveat: starting a business is a personal decision and isn't right for everyone. But we think it's right for more people than you might initially think.

Some reasons *why* you should start a business in business school.

1. It's An Outrageously Ideal Environment.

Many startups fail because they have the wrong team, no access to money or mentorship, or no early audience. You get *all* of these things at school. In spades. You're surrounded by smart, ambitious, and diverse potential co-founders. Most schools have pitch competitions and entrepreneurship programs that provide money and world-class mentorship. Last, simply by being in school you have intimate knowledge of and access to influential early adopters: your fellow students. For whatever reason, too many people (including us) overlook this very obvious fact.

2. It's All Upside With Minimal Risk.

You are winning just by trying. Best case, you build the next Warby Parker. Worst case, it's an awesome learning experience and you just take one of the amazing jobs available to you after school with no gap on your résumé.

3. It Creates Additional Learning Opportunities Outside Of Class.

Starting a business gives you an automatic reason to go deep with professors, speakers, and peers. While you will go to classes and events with some incredibly talented and interesting people, it's often hard to stand out, and it can be too easy to sit on the sidelines. But with a business, you're a different kind of student. You'll have interesting problems, questions, and projects—and an array of smart people who are more than willing to help you figure them out. Go ahead and ask that star professor to be an advisor or to provide feedback on a new product.

4. It Can Make You Money.

We don't need to explain this. If you do this right, you get all the above *and* money flowing in during school. Granted, perhaps you should keep it in the business, but that's up to you.

Okay, you're convinced (maybe). So how do you start a business in school?

In the list that follows, we're not going to cover generic startup advice. There's already a ton of information on this topic that you can research on your own. Our focus is on the specifics of starting a business during an MBA.

1. Don't Go After The Perfect Idea.

It's easy to spend far too long searching for the perfect business with everything you want. That's not the only option. Some of our friends were more practical. They focused on getting an experience—just finding something that had a solid chance of working. This is particularly important in school because you have limited time. For example, renting out photo booths might not seem sexy, but it's practical and provides a ton of learning.

2. Pick Something That Will Appeal To Your Fellow Students.

Finding early adopters is often the hardest part of building a business, but not for you. We've seen students start clothing and food brands that got off the ground through purchases from their classmates.

3. Tell Everyone.

Become a magnet for serendipity. Most schools have a very strong culture of support. Once you're known as the "XYZ person," you'll start to get flooded with connections, support, and information.

4. Don't do it alone.

You're going to be very busy balancing a business with school, not to mention a social life. You're also going to be surrounded by an incredible group of peers and have access to thousands of students in other schools (engineering, undergrad, etc.). Find a partner (or partners). It can only help your business if you can find someone with complementary strengths and the ability to share the workload.

THE TAKEAWAY

Again, starting a business isn't right for everyone. But if you want to create a real-world opportunity to apply your learnings during school—and we definitely think that you should—starting a business may be the way to do it.

PART 4

THE META LAYER

CHAPTER 13

Miscellaneous tips

It feels like 90 percent of coffee chats conclude with the question, "Is there anything else I should know?" And although a more impactful way to scan for missing information does exist (which we'll return to next Chapter), this open-ended question has led to a grab bag of random smaller tips and thoughts that we'll share here.

1. Logistics

- If your school doesn't let you keep your @edu email forever, consider setting it up as an alias for a personal email. That will allow you to keep using the .edu even after you graduate, which can be invaluable in contacting fellow alum.
- Save all your files. Beyond helping with your strategy to intentionally remember learnings (as discussed in the section "How can I remember everything important?"),

this can pay dividends down the road. Even if you don't love some materials now, they could be a helpful resource in the future. You'll be asked, "Have you ever done XYZ?" And you'll remember you did a case study on it in your marketing class. Semesters and dates blur together, so organize your folders in a way that will make this type of search easy. One tip is to make sure every file coming onto your computer is saved automatically, ensuring you can search for anything that escapes your portfolio or note-taking approach.

2. Social life

- Find people different from you as well as those you naturally gravitate towards. If you play pickup basketball, it'll mostly be with American dudes. That's fine, but maybe also try broadening your horizons through classes and clubs. Because schools focus on creating a class of diverse backgrounds, this may be one of the most interesting and curated groups you'll ever be a part of. How can you maximize your own learning and perspective development?
- Quick caveat: Schools like to champion the diversity of the student bodies they create. However, socioeconomic diversity will likely be (sorely) lacking. Many of your classmates will be wealthy. Be mindful of the blinders this creates.

3. Academics

- Treat professors like your parents' friends. Be respectful but casual. Especially in the US, the culture with professors is pretty relaxed, and you'll get more out of the relationship if you proceed like this than if you maintain a formal rigidity.

4. Personal life

- Travel small. Traveling is a big part of the experience for many students. Big trips get the most attention but are typically expensive and less personal. You don't need to do every trip, and you definitely don't need to spend a ton of money on the trips you take. You only have two years on campus, so think strategically about how often you leave. For us, it was more meaningful to take a few trips with smaller groups. Visiting Colombia with two hundred MBA students didn't really feel like visiting Colombia—it felt like partying with two hundred MBA students, but in South America. Fun and unique in its own way. But know what you want.

- Read, run, climb! Whatever your passion is, pick it back up. The next few years will be unique. As an adult (maybe?) with defined passions, it's easy to find a group of like-minded individuals. Plus, the school environment provides nearly unlimited resources. Do you, say, like sports? You'll once again have access to a gym and be able to regularly get ten people to run up and down a basketball court. Like reading? Make a book club. Do you have a passion for something else? You may have let your passions fade while pursuing work, but now it's time to lean back in. School is a special time—embrace it.

CHAPTER 14

What to ask
and how to ask it

There are two basic elements to a successful coffee chat strategy: a) the people you talk to, and b) the questions you ask. To that end, we wanted to take a beat to discuss how you can improve the coffee chat itself.

As mentioned, we've both been on lots of calls that end with a thank you and the same open-ended question: "Thanks so much, and do you have any other advice for me?"

That's a huge missed opportunity. Open-ended questions invite general answers that often have little relevance to your individual situation. In addition to asking important questions (which we'll return to in a moment) and saying thank you, you should always end each coffee chat with two specific questions that will help you get the most from it.

1. The Best Two Questions to End With

The person you're talking to probably knows at least ten things that could materially improve your MBA experience. You may be able to guess a few of these things beforehand; maybe you checked out their background and noticed that they are heavily involved in an interest of yours (say, the autonomous driving club). Use your time to dig into that. But you can't guess them all. Plus, depending on the length of your conversation, you might only have time to ask one or two questions. Especially if you're asking follow-up questions, the time goes by quickly.

So you need a way to quickly reveal important information you're missing out on. To elicit this, we recommend asking:

"What didn't I ask that I should have?"

This is a great way to solicit their "best advice" that you might not otherwise have gotten. Be aware: the answers to this question can be long, so make sure you budget some time for this. Simple enough.

The second question is key and, importantly, invites more discussion. If there is one question you should always ask (Every. Single. Person.), it is:

"Is there anyone else I should talk to about X?"

(Or phrased more strongly: "Is there anyone you would be willing to introduce me to to talk about X?")

Always try to get as specific as possible (e.g., "Is there anyone I should talk to about starting a healthcare company while in school?").

The person you're talking to is most likely part of an insanely and magically large and helpful network. They probably know at least two or three people who share nearly 100 percent of your interests and may already have your dream career. This is how you get introduced to them.

This is also an easy way to judge how good you are at these chats. If the person you're talking to doesn't connect you with anyone, then one of two things is happening. One, you may have been unpleasant to talk with and they don't want anyone else to experience what they just did. Two, they are the rare MBA student with a small network and no one to refer you to. It's probably the first one. Use this signal as a chance to get better at chatting. That's okay—these conversations often feel a bit unnatural at first. And it's good practice for interview season.

This brings up another important topic. How do you ask better questions in general?

2. Ask Better Questions by Pursuing "Bad News"

As we mentioned at the beginning of this section, Admits too often ask open-ended or upbeat 'soft' questions like: What have you loved the most? What are your friends like? What was your favorite class? All of these questions are implicitly asking: What's great about the experience?

This approach will generate good soundbites, but we recommend a different approach if you want candid responses (and who doesn't?).

That being the case, you should also consider asking things like: What did you hate about the experience? What do you regret not doing? What was your biggest mistake? Don't be afraid of adding in these slightly more uncomfortable and personal questions. They help for a few different reasons.

First, they can protect against cognitive biases. The person you are talking to has invested a lot of time and money into their program. They want to believe everything is great, and that's what they'll almost always tell you unless you make a deliberate effort to dig past that bias.

Second, we find these questions better identify real learnings. Most schools will provide a lot that you love. But there will also be some things that aren't so great. While most people don't enjoy talking about these, wouldn't you want to hear about them in advance?

Third, this kind of "real talk" will help you understand, in concrete terms, what that person or their friends did—and how things turned out as a result. As much as possible, you want to minimize conjecture about the overall experience. Just remember that their personal background, their unique goals, and a variety of other factors will heavily influence their feelings regarding their MBA.

3. Plan and Prepare the Most Useful Questions

One final bit of advice is to add some structure to your set of questions. No single coffee chat will answer all of them, so each chat should have a specific purpose. Taken together, they will provide the input you need.

In our view, there are six "buckets" of MBA life: Personal life, Relationships, Social life, Travel, Academics, and Career. If you don't like these groupings, feel free to create your own. Regardless of how you choose, the key is to have a good organizing framework in order to think through all of your questions.

Here are some insight-producing questions you might ask for each bucket. Use them to tailor your outreach and ask questions that are more relevant—both for yourself and your chatting companion. For all of them, be curious. And don't be afraid to ask follow-up questions: How do you feel about it? Any regrets? Would you suggest this or that?

Personal life

- How do you spend your free time?
- What have you said no to in school?
- What was the best choice you made during school? The worst choice?

Relationships

- How has your relationship changed during school?
- Has your partner been active in the school community? Why or why not? Do they have any regrets about their role?
- How should I prepare my partner for the experience?

Social life

- What's something you're happy you don't do?
- What are some fun things you do each week?
- Do you feel like you've found "your people" in school? When did that happen?
- Is it difficult or competitive to get involved in activities at school? Were there any things that you or a friend wanted to do but couldn't?

Travel

- What trips have you taken/are you planning to take during your MBA?
- What trips do you wish you had taken?
- What trips do you wish you had not taken?
- How did you budget for trips?

Academics

- Who do you know that has particularly loved/hated their time here? Why do they feel this way?
- Would you mind sharing a snapshot of your calendar?
- How do you pick classes?
- Do you minimize/optimize/maximize the academic part of school? How do you do it?

Career

- What's the weirdest job you've seen people do?
- What's one other job you wish you had explored? Why didn't you?
- Do you know people in X career? How did they break into it?

CHAPTER 15

How to find
people to chat with

At this point, some of you are ready to plow ahead and start hitting up inboxes. Some of you may have absorbed everything written so far but are wondering how to get started. These final sections are for you.

Let's start with how to build up your coffee chat list, which focuses on finding warm intros and parlaying each conversation into subsequent connections.

1. Start With "Toehold" Groups That You've Already Met.

Generally speaking, there are three good groups you can tap into if you want to find someone to talk with: personal connections, people you met while applying for admission to/visiting your school, and alumni that have contacted you to congratulate you on admission.

If you've been admitted to a school, chances are you know at least one person from one of these groups. They're the logical place to start. Personal connections are great for asking 'dumb' questions. You can trust they'll give it to you straight and that they have your best interests in mind. Plus, you're almost guaranteed a response. However, not everyone has access to this group. And if you're looking to pivot to a new career or gain a new perspective, they might be less valuable.

Anyone you met while applying is also fair game. They may be slightly less likely to respond because they probably meet a lot of people throughout the year. It's important to be respectful and succinct when you reach out. Make it easy for them. Start by asking for a phone call or, if meeting in-person, go to them.

Lastly, most schools have their alumni reach out to people who have been accepted to congratulate them on admission. Often, these people are matched to you based on mutual career interest or some other commonality. These people are an underutilized resource. They reached out to you—so the ball is in your court, and it's up to you to keep the conversation going or to reignite it. Obviously, the value of this resource depends on the school making a suitable match. If these contacts work in an area of your interest, though, you'll want to be a bit more careful. You might recruit with this person in a few months, so keep that in the back of your mind when you're thinking up dumb jokes to impress them with.

2. *Next, Reach Out To Current Students With Overlapping Interests.*

For cold outreach, current students are usually a better bet than alumni. Their school-related issues are immediately relevant and their experiences are fresh. That said, we don't suggest you start by emailing students directly.

Let the school help funnel you to the right places. For career-related questions, give the career center a call so you can explain what you're looking for and ask what connections they might be able to make.

For just about anything else, most clubs on campus have active leaders and the ability to quickly contact their members. They also usually publish their club email addresses and have several officers monitoring it. Just search "School + Interest + Club."

3. Hit Up Alumni Via Linkedin Or Other Publicly Available Sources.

Most school communities are extremely supportive. They tout incredibly high response rates to cold outreach. Truthfully, you might be able to reach out to pretty much anyone at the school and get some help. But people are busy.

We recommend targeting people with two degrees of overlap. The first is your shared school. The second might be an industry of interest, a city you live in, or something else about your background. Just about anything can be a starting point.

That's a ton of options. But you really only need one. Whoever you speak with, be sure to ask good questions (Chapter 14) and end every conversation by asking, "Is there anyone else I should talk with?" Do this and you'll quickly be inundated with coffee chats, new friends, and valuable connections.

The End

That's it! That's all we've got :).

Hopefully this was helpful. If it wasn't, remember you can email us at adam@mbacoffeechats.com to let us know what we got wrong and how you think we can improve.

Obviously, everything in this book is subjective and based on our own experiences. We encourage you to disagree and commit to an alternate path. That intentionality will lead to a wonderful MBA experience, regardless if you agree with our viewpoint.

We believe collecting a variety of perspectives via coffee chats is the best way to maximize the quality of your time in school. Especially in the months before you matriculate, you have a clean slate and a mind unaffected by the swirl of MBA life. It's a great time to identify and refine your priorities.

Remember, there's no need to reinvent the wheel. The thousands of people who have come before you have already figured out how to have an amazing and valuable MBA experience. It's up to you to ask strong questions and take an intentional approach. By reading this book, you've already started.

Congratulations again on getting into school—we are so excited for you. Always feel free to reach out if you have questions (www.mbacoffeechats.com). And if this was helpful, please pay it forward—have lots of coffee chats and be open to pass on your own perspective. We're sure someone will appreciate it.